Instrument Rated Christian

by
Roy and Margaret Hicks

HARRISON HOUSE
Tulsa, Oklahoma

Unless otherwise indicated,
all Scripture quotations are taken from
the *King James Version* of the Bible.

10th Printing

Instrument Rated Christian
ISBN 0-89274-334-4
Formerly entitled *Ready or Not, Here Comes Trouble*
ISBN 0-89274-148-1
Copyright © 1980 by Roy H. Hicks
P.O. Box 4113
San Marcos, California 92069

Published by Harrison House, Inc.
P.O. Box 35035
Tulsa, Oklahoma 74153

Contents

Introduction

Our Lord Jesus set wonderful examples for us by being prepared for the troubles and tests that He was to face.

He prepared for His entry into ministry by fasting for forty days.

He prepared for His death in the Garden of Gethsemane.

Being prepared is not simply a confession of, "Trouble will never knock at my door!"

Pastors are constantly picking up the pieces of broken lives of people who thought tragedy would never come their way . . . hence they were not prepared for it.

The authors prayerfully hope that this book will help you to be ready by being an "instrument rated Christian," one that is prepared to take on the storms of life, even as Jesus did.

May the reading of this book help you to know a great truth: *If you wait until trouble comes to find a scripture to help you . . . you may have waited too long.*

David Ingles says it very ably, in an easy to be remembered way: **"If your mouth will feed your heart faith when you don't need it, then your heart will feed your mouth faith when you do."**

1

Instrument Rated

Pilot: (to tower) "This is Cessna #47831 calling Oakland Center. Can you read me?"

Tower: (to pilot) "I read you #47831. Go ahead."

Pilot: "I need to declare an emergency. I have hit a fog bank. It is bigger than I thought and I'm lost."

Tower: "Are you instrument rated?"

Pilot: "No, I'm not."

Tower: "Squawk 7700 . . . Ok, I have you on radar. I will give you some turns that will bring you back into the traffic pattern to the airport. Turn right heading 240 . . . good. Now turn left heading 180 . . . good. Turn right heading 255 . . . ."

. . . Suddenly, breaking in, the words of the pilot . . .

"I believe I am in a spin and going down."

These were his last words. He was killed in that crash. If he had been instrument rated and able to fly in adverse circumstances, these maneuvers would have been merely routine. The radar controller would have brought him safely in.

Christian: "Thank you for seeing me today, Pastor. I know you are busy and I should have come in sooner."

Pastor: "I am always happy to assist you whenever I can. What can I do for you?"

Christian: "Lately I have been feeling as though I am in a fog bank. I seem to have lost direction. I'm confused."

Pastor: "I have been missing you in church lately. You do still believe in God and in His goodness, don't you?"

Christian: "Oh, yes, I know He is there somewhere, and I used to feel Him near; but since my marriage broke up and I lost my job, things have been getting darker. I've even thought of taking my life."

Pastor: "Have you been praying and reading your Bible?"

Christian: "No, not really . . . I pick it up and lay it down."

This story ends the same way the true story of the pilot ended . . . in disaster and defeat. Had the Christian been "instrument rated" in his Bible knowledge, these storms (difficulties) would have been handled. His heavenly Father, the Lord Jesus and the Holy Spirit, his "heavenly radar," would have guided him through all of his emergencies.

The lost pilot and the troubled Christian have something in common. Both could sail along life's pathway smoothly until the storm came. They were not ready for the troubles they encountered. They are typical of many who do not make that special effort, who do not have that special dedication to prepare for that which all will inevitably face . . . the storms of life.

There are literally thousands of pilots who learn to fly a small plane. They can take off, maneuver, and land it. They can do this successfully as long as they can see where they are going. They can find their way, going by the land marks, rivers, mountains, lakes and highways. But when they are socked in by storms and cannot see, they will be overcome by *vertigo* . . . as was the aforementioned pilot.

Vertigo can be illustrated in this way. If you were to blindfold a person, sit him in a revolving chair and spin him around and around for several moments, then stop the chair and ask him which direction he was spinning, he could not tell you with certainty.

You see, there is a sensitive device in our heads that can be likened to a caprenter's level. The force of the motion of spinning will send the "bubble" as far as it can go to one side. When it can go no further, it begins to return . . . even though the person may still be spinning in the same direction.

Thus, he has the sensation of stopping and beginning to spin in the opposite direction. But it is only a sensation and in reality he has never changed direction! If he were not blindfolded and could see, he could ignore those sensations and would have no difficulty in knowing which direction he was going.

Pilots know that it takes many hours of training in simulated storm conditions to develop the ability to confidently go entirely by the directions of the instruments and be able to ignore the sensations of vertigo.

Recently, a pilot told me that the more he HAD to depend on his instruments, the more CONFIDENCE he had in them.

Likewise, the average Christian can fare well until the storms of life envelop him and the winds of trouble blow him off course. Just as with the pilot and his training, it requires extensive training in Scripture for the Christian to be instrument rated and be able to survive. Intensive saturation training in his instrument, the Bible, will prepare him to ignore his senses and feelings and to live boldly and confidently by the Word.

Preparing for the inevitable trials without fear is one of our greatest challenges. Ever since Adam and Eve fell in the garden of Eden, we have been constantly surrounded by millions of germs and viruses; confronted by the ever present danger of accident and the dangers that lurk and wait to attack.

We are not beyond all of this just because we are believers in Jesus and His resurrection. *There must be constant input of the Word and faith* so we will be ready for this dark and ominous cloud that hangs over all of us, waiting to test and oppose every step we take. (Read Ephesians 6:10-17.)

Let us talk again of the parallel of the pilot and the Christian. As a regularly licensed pilot prepares to fly his craft to his destination, he must first check the weather. Many times this is very difficult because weather reports are very late. Atmospheric conditions can change rapidly.

The regular pilot charts a visual route. That is, he must be able to see the ground at all times. He must also be certain that his flight takes him into fair weather, and that he will have access to many airports along the way in case he happens upon a storm. Many pilots, in their efforts to steer around one storm, end up in another one that is worse. This is one reason we read in the newspapers of so many small plane crashes. Very seldom does a small plane crash happen because of mechanical failure. *It is usually pilot error.* This is why it is so important for a pilot of a small plane to get his instrument rating, especially if he lives in an area where storms are frequent—unless of course, he flies only in fair weather.

When a regular privately licensed pilot takes off, he must constantly turn aside from any confrontation with the storm. The instrument rated pilot can fly directly into it. He can be totally socked in, watch his instruments and fly along completely without fear.

In order to do this, he must have many hours of rigid training in simulated storm conditions. Trouble, to him, is normal. He has gone through it many times, knows exactly what to do in every emergency. He knows how to use his radio and to constantly receive help from the radar centers. He knows how to stay on the radio beams that are criss-crossing the skies for his safety. The mountain that looms up suddenly before him, shows up on the controller's radar scope. The controller can guide the straying plane far around the obstacle if necessary.

Remember, if a pilot is not instrument rated, it is illegal for him to be in a storm! He cannot be in bad weather. He cannot have the help of millions of dollars worth of radar and personnel to help him, because he has not taken the time, or felt it was important to do his homework and be prepared.

To be ready for the storms of life, i.e. sickness, accidents, financial disaster, marital difficulties, means that one must BE PREPARED BY SPENDING HOURS IN THE WORD. **This is the instrument of the Christian walk.** Great familiarity with it is necessary if the Christian is to be "certified" to navigate all of the storms of life.

When a regularly licensed pilot, who has his private license, desires to go to the instrument rated license, he must apply and be ready to begin his hours and hours of study. Then an instructor is assigned to him who will accompany him on his training missions.

The instructor will place a hood (a long-billed cap) on the pilot's head so that all the pilot can see is the instrument panel in front of him. This is all he could see if he were actually flying in storm conditions or a fog. This is done after the craft is in the air a few hundred feet. A course is set and the pilot in training must work his instruments and radio, doing many turns, being able to come to an airport and bring the plane within a few feet of the landing strip.

He must do all of this *without* ever LOOKING to see where he is, *without* ever having any CONFIRMATION of any of his senses.

This simulated blindness, causing confusion to the average person, is soon overcome by disciplined training. The flights "under the hood" (as this procedure is called) become merely routine flights.

What happens when an unprepared Christian is plunged into darkness by the trials of life?

He questions what is happening. Everything was going so well—all he could see ahead was fair weather!

This bewildered saint soon loses direction and perception because he has not been in the Word. He has not been taught to believe, *regardless of what he sees or feels*. He soon gets discouraged, backslides, and sometimes even blames God and is swallowed up in bitterness.

Perhaps the best illustration of this in the Bible is found in John chapter 20. The story is related of Jesus' encounter with the disciple Thomas. Thomas had not been present when Jesus suddenly appeared to His disciples after His resurrection. So when Thomas returned, the disciples related how Jesus had come to them through the closed door.

The last time Thomas had seen Jesus was at the crucifixion. He had, no doubt, seen His dead body taken from the cross and placed in the tomb. If ever a man was dead, it was Jesus, and Thomas knew it. Thomas argued with the disciples about the impossibility of Jesus being there with them. He may even have suggested that, because of fear, they were hallucinating! He said, "I will not believe until I have seen Him and thrust my hand into His side."

A few days later, Jesus reappeared and said to Thomas, "Be not faithless, but believing." He invited Thomas to thrust his hand into His side. Thomas fell to his knees and said, "My Lord and my God."

Then Jesus said these significant words, "Thomas, because thou hast seen Me, thou hast believed. Blessed are they that have not seen, and yet have believed."

Jesus, in this passage, pronounced a great blessing on all who will believe without their natural senses being involved . . . upon all of those **CHRISTIANS WHO ARE INSTRUMENT RATED— those who do not live by what they see or feel, but by what the Bible, our instrument book, says.**

While it is true that He was constrained to allow Thomas to have that painful experience of thrusting his hand into the gaping hole in His side . . . He desires so much that we believe, that He will tolerate our painful experiences with trouble without condemnation. You can borrow the money. There is nothing wrong in going to the doctor. Jesus will do everything He can do to help us. But there is something far better than these experiences.

Get that training in His Word that will put you in that rare category of not depending upon the feel of being healed, of not depending on money in the bank . . . but of childlike faith in trusting Him for what you do not see or feel. Praise Him because you have all of heaven behind you . . . and for you. *He is watching over you with heavenly radar.* You will not fly into that craggy mountain top. You will not fly off course, because you have been a disciplined Christian. You have paid the price of study and waiting on God. You are ready for any trouble that says, "Ready or not, here I come!"

Second Timothy 2:15 says "Study and be eager and do your utmost to present yourself to God approved (tested by trial) a workman who has no cause to be ashamed, correctly analyzing and accurately dividing, rightly handling and skilfully teaching the word of truth" (*The Amplified Bible*).

2

Instrument Rated For Trouble

Almost all Christians can sail along smoothly, until trouble comes. Jesus said, "In the world you will have tribulation, but be of good cheer; I have overcome the world" (John 16:33).

Job says, *"Yet man is born unto trouble, as the sparks fly upward . . . He shall deliver thee in six troubles, yea in seven there shall no evil touch thee . . . In famine he shall redeem thee from death and in war from the power of the sword . . . At destruction and famine thou shalt laugh"* (Job 5:7,19,20,22).

Paul talked about troubles in 2 Corinthians 4:8-9: *"We are troubled on every side, yet not distressed; we are perplexed, but not in despair; Persecuted, but not forsaken; cast down, but not destroyed."*

Troubles? Yes, they will come. You will be tested, but provision for deliverance is made.

"He shall call upon me, and I will answer him; I will be with him in trouble; I will deliver him and honour him" (Psalm 91:15).

Some people dwell only on troubles. Some dwell only on deliverance. Perhaps the balance is to know that troubles will come to us, the trial of our faith will come, but to be ready for the storm . . . to be able to fly your course directly into the storm without fear does take preparation, and this we MUST do. Deliverance will come . . . but PREPARATION is paramount if we are to successfully navigate the stormy times.

I have heard people say, "If I had known this was going to happen, I would have been ready for it."

Devastating, shocking news not only catches some people totally unprepared for the present, but has a shattering effect upon the rest of their lives.

Some people never do recuperate from that telephone call when someone announces to them the death of a loved one; a wife hears her husband say, "I'm in love with someone else." Maybe a call from the police station—a voice informing you that your child has been caught in a drug bust. A tearful, teenage daughter, sobbing out her confession of pregnancy.

All of these situations, and many more, hurtful and tormenting incidences are the voice of trouble saying, "Ready or not, here I come!"

We CAN BE ready. We WILL BE ready.

Just as the pilot of a plane must be ready for that storm that will come against the path he is travelling . . . so must we diligently prepare for the storm that awaits us. We do not seek trouble. We do not fear it. *But when it comes and knocks on our door, let it be FAITH that answers.*

When someone comes to me with a problem, I usually ask, "Can you qoute me a verse of Scripture to cover this?" Often they cannot do it. The fact of the matter is, if they knew what the Scripture said concerning their problem . . . they probably would not be seeking help.

If someone asks me if she should go ahead with scheduled surgery, I usually answer, "Yes, you should."

You will say, "Now wait a minute, I thought you were a faith teacher!"

True, I teach faith, but I have learned to meet people *where they are*. If they were ready to trust God for that need, they would not be asking someone what to do. They cannot ride on someone's faith other than their own.

Mature Christians often cause, unknowingly, their loved ones and friends to act presumptuously by compelling them up to their level of faith, rather than permitting them to act according to their own faith at the present time.

A good flying instructor will not put a student into difficult maneuvers before he is ready.

May this book not only assure you that you can take on the storms of life with confidence, but that you can fly right through them and above them where the sun is shining brightly and all is clear. (Read author's book, *He Who Laughs . . . Lasts . . . And Lasts . . . And Lasts . . .*)

First Corinthians 10:11 alerts us to this great need of getting ready to experience things that no other people before us have ever experienced. It says, ". . . upon whom the ends of the world are come." W. E. Vine translates it, "In whose lives the climax of the ages has been reached." Our generation will experience all the diabolical trouble satan can generate. It will be so severe that only the very elect will be able to survive.

We must be ready, armed with God's Word as a two-edged sword coming out of our mouths.

3

Instrument Rated For Discouragement

The author has taken surveys of many congregations and groups and discovered that up to 90% of all Christians freely admit to getting depressed or discouraged.

Recently an article in a local paper related what happens to people when they succumb to discouragement. People quit their jobs and in so doing will forfeit many years of seniority. They will walk away from a fairly healthy marriage. Young people will take to the streets and to drugs because of the terrible storms of depression. Sickness, with diverse symptoms that baffle the physician, will result from these attacks. The most extreme depression sometimes ends in suicide.

Realizing that this attack comes to us all, ready or not, I thought I should have at least one message to help the oppressed one. When I set about to look up scriptures that deal with depression, I discovered that the word was not in the Bible.

How could I have a message on depression if the word is not in the Bible?

I turned to Webster's Dictionary to see how the word was defined so I could find a comparable word in the Bible. The word "depressed" means "to be flattened vertically or dispirited." (Now you know why you don't want to get up in the morning!)

The word in the Bible that answers to this definition is "heaviness." It expresses sorrow, burden, and something hard to endure. We have all had this feeling of heaviness when we have been depressed.

Proverbs 12:25 says, "Heaviness in the heart of man maketh it stoop: but a good word maketh it glad." The Jerusalem Bible translated this to read, "Worry makes a man's heart heavy, a kindly word makes it glad." J.P.S. translates the word, "heavy" to mean care. YLT translates it to mean sorrow of the heart; and Berkeley used the word, "anxiety."

This kind of trouble is awaiting you daily. There will always be something you could worry about that would bring depression.

The toughest battles you will ever fight will be those with your own mind.

I believe it was for this reason that the Lord said to me, "Teach my people that they cannot out-think the devil." (He could have said "out-worry.")

"That is true, Lord," I said. "Satan is too intelligent and experienced for us. What can we do then?"

He said, "You can out-talk him because he cannot answer you back."

I had never thought about that. Satan cannot speak out loud. Thus, when you say, "Satan you are a liar and the father of lies," he cannot answer you back. You will always win every one-sided conversation!

Notice that the answer to heaviness, brought on by anxiety and worry is, "a good word maketh it glad." **Speaking aloud is the answer!** The most effective word to speak, of course, is the Word of God. (In another chapter we cover the areas that cause worry.)

Just remember, you cannot "out-worry" worry. You must speak aloud the Word of God and that alone will dominate the mind and stop the worry. The more you talk, the less satan can say.

In Isaiah 61:3c the Bible says, ". . . the garment of praise for the spirit of heaviness." Here depression or discouragement is a spirit. It is a direct, diabolic attack of the enemy, intended to destroy you. The thought in the Hebrew sense is to "put out the fire, grow dull."

Someone has suggested that satan pays a personal visit to every Christian once a year. Whether or not he comes in person, or sends emissaries, we know that if he can get us discouraged, depressed, heavy hearted . . . then he has us obeying him instead of God!

What is one to do in this situation of depression caused by satan?

PUT ON THE GARMENT OF PRAISE! Begin to sing praises to God. Rejoice before the Lord. It is a time to reverse what your senses tell you. Do not go by your feelings, or you will go down for sure.

Just as the sensations of vertigo will mislead the plane pilot, so will your feelings mislead you and you will lose your direction. Your feelings will cause you to think about self . . . to feel sorry for yourself. I call this having a "pity party." You begin to believe that you have it tougher than others; that breaks happen for others but never for you. You even feel that people who say they love you don't really mean it.

This pity party can last a lifetime for some. Their face reflects it. Someone has said, "We end up with the face we deserve." A lifetime of giving in to negative feelings and thinking will make indelible lines in your face.

What is the answer to these attacks?

Make yourself change garments!

"To appoint unto them that mourn in Zion, to give unto them beauty for ashes, the oil of joy for mourning, the garment of praise for the spirit of heaviness; that they might be called trees of righteousness, the planting of the Lord, that he might be glorified" (Isaiah 61:3).

WE ARE TO PUT ON THE GARMENT OF PRAISE AND WORSHIP!

Satan, who fell by reason of his pride, cannot stay around when someone else is receiving praise and honor. The spirit of heaviness will leave every time when you begin to praise your God. The spirit of heaviness will fall off like a cloak. The weight will leave . . . the pity party will turn into a scene of gladness.

When one becomes a worshiper of God, one who worships at home as well as at church, many beautiful things begin to happen.

When you truly worship God in spirit and in truth, God then is seeking you . . . John 4:23. I would rather have God seeking me and attending to my welfare than my seeking Him. He knows who I am and where I am, at all times.

Teach yourself to become a true worshiper of the Lord Jehovah.

Another experience of heaviness or depression that comes, ready or not, is the heaviness referred to in 1 Peter 1:6, "Wherein ye greatly rejoice, though now for a season, if need be, ye are in heaviness through manifold temptations."

This kind of heaviness is a result of being in a fallen, rebellious, degenerate world that is in the control of satan. Second Corinthians 4:4 says he is the god of this world. He blinds the minds of those who believe not.

Our daily contacts in the every day exercise of living with unbelievers will cause feelings of frustration and depression. It is unavoidable and we cannot escape these emotions.

The tragedies broadcast into our homes, from far and near, through all of the news media will cause us to feel heavy hearted . . . to have great compassion for those involved. Whenever this happens, determine that the season will be short.

Do not misunderstand . . . I do not say we are to be callous or uncaring. Do everything you can for the sorrowing; give of your substance; pray for them; care for them. But you cannot make their load lighter by going around with your own heart heavy.

Determine the season will be short by giving praise and thanks unto God that you are saved. Rejoice that your name is written in heaven.

If more of God's people would ACT like God's people, then more people would want to BECOME God's people! This is why Philippians 4:4 says, "Rejoice in the Lord always." We are commanded to be a happy people.

If you are an instrument rated Christian you will rejoice, regardless of what you see or feel. You will guide your craft according to the instrument, the Word. Give heed to the voice of the controller, your God, and you cannot go down. You can go through that storm because you will do what God says.

Act according to His Word and not your feelings!

Never again will you have a depressed day, a heavy day, or a "stoopy" day. You will experience only rich, full, satisfying days because you know how to sail through the storm and out into the sunlight of God's love.

This chapter on heaviness and depression could be lengthened into a full book. Depressed people are all around us every day. We read it in their faces and hear it from their lips.

If anyone should live above this, it is the Christian, whose source is the Lord, the Supreme One, the Alpha and Omega, the beginning and the end.

Depression that originates from worry and stress of life or from a personal attack of satan or as a result of just every day living in the devil's world . . . is a subtle attack upon your soul.

Be alert to the *first* sign of worry or a feeling of heaviness. Recognize the pity party for what it is. Be ready for that time when you will doubt that someone who says he loves you, really means it. Be mindful of a creeping doubt about God's love and care for you.

Be ready, by being prepared. Take your hours under the hood when you have an instructor by your side to help you. Know who you are in Christ. Worship and praise continually. You can live free from discouragement and depression.

When an instructor is teaching a new student to fly, he constantly reminds him to keep the nose of the plane up. (New students are likely to keep the nose down so they can SEE where they are going. Also, the plane has a natural tendency to fall—if you let it.)

Keeping our heads up, our eyes on Jesus, our hearts rejoicing is also our toughest test. It takes effort, but it's worth it.

Remember, you don't always win every fight in the first round . . . sometimes it is a 15 rounder. But hang in there and keep answering the bell. YOU HAVE TO BE VICTORIOUS *if you don't quit* because the fight was FIXED by Jesus a long time ago.

Instrument Rated For Direction

The compass has always been the airplane pilot's best friend. In fact, most planes are equipped with two of them. Not only the pilot, but the experienced hunter will insist on taking a compass when he heads into the deep woods on an expedition.

Seeking direction for our lives is perhaps the Christian's greatest challenge. To know God's will . . . and be in that will . . . is one of the greatest joys in life.

The questions most frequently asked in open Bible discussion are, "How can I know the will of God? How can I be sure and what if I miss it?"

In the book of Acts, chapter 21 verses 11-14, we find a controversy among the saints as to whether or not the Apostle Paul would be in God's will if he continued his journey to Jerusalem. The prophet Agabus took Paul's sash and bound his own hands with it and prophesied that the Jews at Jerusalem would bind Paul in this manner and deliver him to the Gentiles. This prophecy was correct and it happened to Paul as Agabus said.

The confusion was not in the question of God's will . . . but fear for Paul's life.

Here we have a perfect example of letting our emotions, our soulish realm, get in the way of our spirit. It is by our spirit that we comprehend and understand the ways and directions of the Lord.

"For as many as are led by the Spirit of God, they are the sons of God" (Romans 8:14).

God's Spirit works in our human spirit. Our human spirit is born again by God's Spirit. We are not to be led by voices, dreams, fleeces, and prophecies of others. These things can *support* and *confirm* what we sense in our spirit to be God's will, but are never to be the deciding factor.

Many new Christians go around seeking a word from the Lord through a prophet or prophetess. Usually this word sought is not what God wants, but what THEY want. If they do not hear what they want to hear from this person, they will go to another, and another, until they do.

Finding the will and direction from the Lord will be a result of a seeker's *relationship* to the Lord Jesus by the power of the Holy Spirit. If a Christian, not having such a relationship with the Lord Jesus, were to actually receive direction from the Lord through someone else, then it would be very doubtful if they would be close enough to the Lord to carry out His revealed will.

I know of a group of Christians who actually ended up as missionaries in a remote area of the world as a result of "a word from the Lord" from someone else. Not only were they unsuccessful in doing the work of a missionary . . . but the United States Embassy had to pay their fares back home again.

The Jonestown mass suicide of 1978 is a good example of following what someone else believed to be the will of God. Some tragic results have been documented because someone heard a voice. Words came to them from somewhere. They believed them to be God's words and consequently they were led into great error.

Can you believe voices? Not only are Christians admonished to try the spirits to see if they be of God (I John 4:1a); but even an instrument rated pilot must use his knowledge and experience in flying to weigh very carefully what the controller, the man watching a little blip on his radar screen miles away, tells him to do.

A good example of "trying the voices" comes to us in this incident of a few years back. A controller, directing air traffic, called out the identification number of a plane and instructed him to come down to six thousand feet. The controller was in error . . . but the pilot, following his instructions, did as he said . . . and every passenger on the plane perished as it plunged into the side of a mountain. The pilot, regardless of the controller's directions, is responsible to know where he is at all times. The controller is only to *confirm* his position.

I was flying with one of our Christian pilots in a twin-engine craft. The controller in the tower was bringing us in behind a much slower single-engine plane. It was obvious to us that if we followed the controller's instructions, we would fly into the plane ahead of us. We radioed to the tower that we would go around and come back into the landing pattern again.

So it is in things of the spirit. You dare not believe every voice you hear. *You must act out of relationship with Jesus.* Work out your own direction, relying on other members of the Body of Christ to supply help and confirmation.

Here are some guidelines that I trust will be helpful to you in seeking direction for your life.

1. Do not seek for a change when you are already in God's will. For example, if you are doing God's will in studying His Word in Bible College, do not fret over what you are going to do when you get out. This will only frustrate you and interfere with your studies. Simply trust in God with all of your heart and lean not to your own understanding and He will be faithful to guide you at the time of graduation. (Proverbs 3:5-6.)

This will also help young mothers. You are already doing God's first will. When those children are raised and have homes of their own and you have fulfilled that calling, there will be more time for other pursuits. Keep the balance between being a mother and having a ministry.

2. Do not seek to do something great. Our emotions often lead us to fancy ourselves doing great exploits. No great person, highly used by the Lord ever sought to accomplish great goals. It was something that resulted from their obedience to God in what they were already doing.

Billy Graham never sought God by saying, "Lord, make me a great world-known evangelist." He, as an evangelist, was already doing God's will.

Aimee Semple McPherson never sought to be a great evangelist in her day. She started out by washing dishes and playing the organ in a tent crusade.

Many pastors of large churches never sought to be where they are.

Pat Robertson never dreamed that by merely obeying God in a small way, that God would use him to bring forth the first Christian broadcasting network with around-the-world TV coverage for Christian programming.

Remember Matthew 6:33 says, *"But seek ye first the kingdom of God, and his righteousness; and all these things shall be added unto you."*

3. **Do not be presumptuous in praying for God's will.** David prayed that God would spare him from this sin—presumption. Being presumptuous in seeking God's will is a result of overestimating your talents. This is also the sin of pride. I heard it said of one individual, "If you could buy him for what he is worth and sell him for what he thinks he is worth, you would be rich."

Romans 12:3 admonishes us "not to think more highly of ourselves than we ought to think." Do not be led into this error and sin.

4. **Cultivate a deep personal relationship with Jesus now.** If you are a salesman, a clerk, an engineer, an architect, etc. remember, David had a beautiful relationship with God while tending sheep . . . and he became a giant-slayer.

5. **Memorize Scripture.** Be a "quoter of the Word"; not in quoting endlessly, but in being able to use it when it will bless others and yourself.

6. **Pray much with the understanding and with the Spirit.** The people who are used by God are much in prayer before the throne. Every true man of God that I know personally, is a man of prayer.

7. **Learn to love people.** Learning to love people the way they are and not the way you might want them to be is a constant challenge to our soulish realm. When you listen to successful men of God, men you wish to emulate, always notice that they have a great love for God and for people.

8. **Be very forgiving and repentant.** God loves the contrite heart. Never talk about people's weaknesses and faults. Be quick to defend them when others speak of their faults. Remember, love always believes the best and rejects the worst.

9. **Learn to rely on the inner man.** I have also heard this referred to as a hunch, a feeling, a premonition, a sense of inner peace. The mind is not to be set

aside and ignored; but, on the other hand, you cannot rely completely on the knowledge you have. God leads by the inner man. That inner man is born again by God's Holy Spirit. Thus you have within you, God's Spirit, who is eternal. That Eternal Spirit in our human spirit knows all things. Your born-again spirit, by God's Spirit, will lead you and guide you. Learn how to seek God in that honest acknowledgment of all your ways.

God's will and direction is not difficult to know WHEN YOU KNOW HIM. An instrument rated Christian does not go by what he sees or feels, but by what the instrument, God's Word, says.

When Jesus said, "Not my will but thine be done," He already knew God's will. He was rising up against His own weakness as one that was wrapped in human flesh. Most of us already know His will. Let us do it and not worry or fret about the future. He will direct our path.

If you don't know God's will . . . be patient; do the things listed above. Always know that with God's will there will be that great restful peace. And remember: FAITH NEVER STRUGGLES, IT RESTS!

5

Instrument Rated For Marriage

It is with great reluctance that we write this chapter concerning the storm cloud of trouble that is rocking the homes of America. This chapter should not have to be placed in a Christian book. The Christian home, above all others, should be invulnerable to the bad weather of spiritual attack. Not only is the Christian home subjected to this onslaught, but in many places, it is being riddled by the fiery darts of the enemy. Pastors in every place share with us that they are facing this constantly—especially the past five years.

Statistics tell us that the fastest growing group in America is the singles group. It seems that the people of the world who do not claim Jesus as their Lord are better prepared for this devastating storm than the Christian!

I sense that one reason for this is that the Christian, married to a Christian, has a tendency to ignore the warning signs of a deteriorating marriage. Each one seems to believe that the other is an instrument rated Christian and totally able to cope with subtle attacks of the enemy upon the marriage.

Many Christians are not only NOT instrument rated in the Word of God (meaning that they live by faith in the Word and not by feelings or sight) but they do not even make a great effort to keep their personal physical life under control.

The husband has a tendency, after a few years of marriage to the mother of his children, to take her for granted. Isn't she always there when he comes home? Aren't the meals always ready on time? Isn't the house always neat and clean? Isn't she always ready to follow him into the bedroom at his beck and call?

In this error of taking her for granted, we find the little foxes that begin to spoil the vines.

No longer does he eat the good meal she has prepared with appreciation, or notice the neat, clean clothing she lays out for him to wear. He only complains when there is something wrong. He is tired when he comes home from work, sits grumpily in front of the TV for his favorite programs and fusses at the kids . . . becoming a slowly dying martyr to his marriage.

Looking at the other side of the marriage coin, you cannot help but notice the telltale signs surfacing in the wife. Why should she keep her weight down? Why should she make that extra effort to cook a gourmet meal? Or keep a clean house? All she ever hears are complaints. It is no wonder she slowly succumbs to the role of a non-person.

Satan, the tempter, usurper, and destroyer of the home, cannot drive a car, fire a gun or force you to commit suicide. *What he can do is take advantage of your weaknesses and times of discouragement.* These little "cracks in the dam" are all he needs to begin to wear away and erode the substance of a once healthy and happy marriage.

She had never really noticed the neighbor until he began to compliment her on the beautiful lawn and flowers she worked so hard over. She began to dress more attractively, watch her weight. The husband didn't notice, but the neighbor did. What followed has been multiplied time after time.

The husband began to dread to come home to a tired, complaining wife. He found many excuses to work late at the office, which required the services of a secretary. Of course she is a serving, uncomplaining, efficient person. Again, you know the rest.

"But these are Christians," you say. "This ought not to happen!"

The Christian seems to be LESS prepared for the paralyzing, numbing effect of the dropped bombshell of, "I want a divorce, I no longer love you" or "There is something I must tell you, I have found someone else."

These soul shocking pronouncements are often much worse than an announcement of death. Time will heal the wound of separation by death . . . but separation of being left alone in a "love triangle" seems worse than death. There is no purpose in continuing to build. A rejected person is prey for anyone who comes along. Hatred wells up; a spirit of bitterness takes over and a life becomes utterly ruined.

I trust that this subject is not so presented that you will reject the premise upon which it is written. Please do not avert your face and refuse to recognize that this is a chief battle arena of satan in the Church in these last days. Instead, prepare yourself for any attack. Be ready for any event. Do not expect it or anticipate it . . . but be instrument rated in the Word of God for any storm you may ever face—including this one.

Just as an instrument rated pilot is ready for all emergencies by knowing his craft, his instruments, and being highly trained and keeping his rating up, so also can we as Christians be living in full power and capacity and be ready for any emergency.

The spouse will never hear himself, or herself, say, "I don't know what I am going to do."

Even though bad news such as this would catch you unsuspecting, your first love is your Lord and you still have Him. He is the dearest thing in your life. *"For thy Maker is thine husband (spouse)"* (Isaiah 54:5a). He is the one that said, "I will never leave you nor forsake you."

When should you confess these things? When the storm is all about you?

NO. You confess this BEFORE the onslaught, just as the instrument rated pilot prepares himself before the storm. The instrument rated Christian doesn't wait to prepare until the storm of rejection or loneliness comes . . . he begins before it happens. He is constantly saying, "He is my husband . . . my lord . . . my friend. He is number one!"

One day we were flying over some rough terrain in a single-engine plane. I asked the pilot, "What would you do if the engine quit?"

He pointed to a logging road far below and said, "I would head for that." He already knew what he would do, thus he was ready.

You can be ready for ANYTHING, by constantly quoting the great truths of God that apply to your walk with the Lord in all contingencies. Do this and you will be ready for any attack.

Here are some training procedures to keep up your instrument rating regarding your marriage. Inasmuch as the word "family" is only mentioned once in the New Testament, let us draw another simile. Live with your spouse as your brother or sister in the Lord, first. The little courtesies we extend to another Christian ought to be constantly extended within the marriage. You are going to live together as husband and wife for a very short time on earth, but as brother and sister forever.

Taking this a step further, your son is your brother and your daughter your sister.

All of the teaching that the Word gives to us starts, in its application, in the home first . . . teaching such as the following (paraphrased for clarity):

Whosoever wants you to go a mile, go two; If someone hits you on one cheek, turn the other.

If you only love someone that loves you, what does that profit?

God says we are not to come to Him until we have made our differences right between us.

I have made a covenant with my eyes, I will not think about the opposite sex.

Love your enemies. Bless them that harass and torment you.

Do not expect to be rewarded in this life for all you do.

If you do not forgive your spouse, I will not forgive you.

Judge not, criticize not, and you shall not be judged and criticized. How can you find fault with the splinter in the eye of your spouse when you have a two-by-four in your own.

Do unto your spouse as you would desire your mate to do unto you.

Do not withhold your bodies from each other.

Prove your *love* in actions as well as in words.

The joy of the Lord is the strength of the marriage.

Pleasant words are as a honeycomb, sweet to the marriage and health to the home.

Rejoice in the Lord always . . . this means even when the fender gets dented or the meal waits on the table, getting cold.

There is a beautiful word in the Greek for the word "perfection" as it is used in Hebrews 13:21. It is *katartizo* and it is a derivative of *artios* meaning "fresh." It literally means "to keep adjusting and repairing in a fresh way."

A Christian marriage can be the epitome of perfection if we keep making things right—adjusting the little things and repairing the mistakes . . . keeping the marriage fresh by saying, "I love you."

Whether or not you believe that your marriage was made IN heaven . . . now that you are married, it is OF heaven! God said what He had joined together, let no man put asunder. You are brother and sister in Christ forever. Live that way. Keep your instrument rating up high enough to meet even the storm that may endeavor to destroy your home.

6

Instrument Rated For Parenthood

There were four long shelves, all filled with books on subjects having to do with children—how to have them, teach them, love them, discipline them, enjoy them. But as I browsed through book after book, I noticed there was nothing pertaining to that point in time when we, as parents, get to turn our children over to the Lord: time to commit them. Every book I glanced through was filled with excellent guidelines. All were based on the scriptures that are so positive and clear.

"Withhold not correction from the child; for if thou beatest him with the rod, he shall not die. Thou shalt beat him with the rod, and shalt deliver his soul from hell" (Proverbs 23:13-14).

These are two verses of Scripture that leave no uncertainty as to the value of a firm spanking when it is deserved!

If all the *explicit* child training scriptures are flawlessly followed . . . along with the *implicit,* i.e. the wholesomeness and togetherness of a balanced and dedicated Christian home . . . then there can only be one outcome. The children that are the product of such a consistent atmosphere will be strong, Christ-centered individuals. This is a fact.

Proverbs 22:6 assures me that if I train up my child in the way he should go, that when he is old, he will not depart from it.

There is a further step beyond the act of dedication, with which we are familiar. It is the step of COMMITTAL.

The act of committing our children to God at the threshold of maturity is so important. Although we desire to be the perfect parent . . . to always have the right answer or the right measure of discipline; to be generous but not indulgent; to allow privileges but not be permissive . . . though we earnestly seek these balances, let's be honest: there are times when we miss it!

There was perhaps, the time when little Johnny opened the kitchen door and tramped across your freshly-mopped kitchen floor with his muddy feet. Your reaction was not the planned parental response you expected. Or the time Mary found your new cosmetics and slathered it on her already rosy cheeks and pink lips . . . almost emptying the $10.00 size kit you squeezed out of the grocery money. You knew you should act in discipline and not react . . . but did you?

Multiply these occasions by the tens of times these emergencies happened. Did you always respond the way you wanted to?

Your son, a new driver, dented the fender on your late-model car. What complicates the discipline here is that you knew in your heart you should have said "no" when he asked for the keys in the first place—a wrong decision.

Space in this chapter would not allow for the reciting of all the incidences where we've heard parents say, "I blew it. I didn't handle that right!"

We have not always been the perfect parents. There has to be a covering for our sincere, but sometimes faulty attempts at parenthood. I believe we have it in the concept of committal.

The inspiration that triggered my desire to write this chapter came from an article I read that referred to what the author called "ferocious motherhood." Some thoughts similar to ones contained in the article had been in my mind for some time. When I mentioned to my son that I might try to write something on it he said, "Why not write a chapter and call it Motherhood/ smotherhood and Fatherhood/botherhood!"

The challenge of raising children with certain boundaries . . . yet allowing them to develop as strong, capable individuals is a strong one. When a baby is born into a household, he needs constant care and endless attention. We hold him, change him, feed him, burp him, rock him, bathe him, wipe his nose, etc. The constant care becomes a *cycle of involvement.* The temptation to stay involved when he has come to the place where we need to *commit* him, is an intense one!

You have filled his life with all the firm and loving training you are capable of doing. There is nothing you can tell him about basic Christian life that you have not told him over and over. At this point, your instructions and repeated advice could become endless nagging . . . and could cause a breach in your relationship that could have potential of becoming a great gulf. There is no way you can go back and relive or do over any part of your experience. It is time to commit him to the Lord. He must stand before God through his own relationship with Him.

You will say, "At what age should this be done?"

There are too many variables to rigidly state an age. Some children are very mature at 16 years of age, others are slower in maturing.

Committing them to the Lord does not mean forsaking them. *COMMITTING* (2 Timothy 1:12) *is acknowledging to the Father that you have done the best you were capable of doing as Christian parents and now you are ready to trust Him for all of their future.* **You will still be there if they turn to you in need.**

You do not *cop out* in compromise of your standards and values. The discipline of your home remains intact. But you will not occupy the place of a nagger or a continual fault-finder.

You commit them. You now turn those energies that have been consumed in the doing for them as babies and children, into prayer time. You are there as one who is very open and available whenever that young person looks for someone to confide in.

Second Timothy 1:12 says that He is able to keep that which we commit to Him.

Committal can be likened to the writing of a letter. We write the salutation, the body of the letter, the ending, and even a p.s. We address the envelope, affix a stamp, lick and seal the envelope. And in all of this, the letter is not committed to the postal service. When we walk to the corner mail box and drop it in the slot . . . then it is committed! We cannot get our hands on it again until it reaches its destination.

How many times have we made committals! We sincerely believed we were committing a person or a burden to the Lord . . . and then later discovered that act of committal had been just that—an act! We were right back where we started, worrying and anxious.

We have a lovely daughter named Lori. She is now 22 years of age. She loves Jesus. During her teenage years she, like many other young people during the tumult and confusion of the early 1970's, was shaken in her Christian experience. She spent the better part of two years in a miserable state of wanting to "follow the crowd" on the outside . . . and crying inside because of the hurt she was inflicting on us and on Jesus.

My husband and I had dedicated her, once and for all, to the Lord when she was a baby. Now we were to learn what it is to be instrument rated in trusting the promises of God in everyday living.

Jeremiah 31:16 promises that our children will come again from the land of the enemy. The walk of faith . . . being instrument rated . . . is learning that we are not any more *encouraged* by the positive happenings than we are *discouraged* by the negative responses. Faith says, "God said it. I believe it" . . . and it doesn't matter whether circumstances are good or bad.

We sought God. His words to us were plain and direct. *One*—make her to know above everything else that you love her. *Two*—do not nag. Continual scolding and complaining will only aggravate the situation. She knows what is right. *Three*—commit her to Me.

We had to learn what true committal is.

In a former book, *Praying Beyond God's Ability*, we dealt with the word "grace" as it is used in prayer. Grace not only means the unmerited favor of God, but also means the operational power of God, or mountain-moving power. Once parents make this act of committal of that son or daughter, they can continue in spiritual ministry by speaking grace in prayer for them.

We had to come to the place of complete relinquishment to the ministering of His will. In a sense, we echoed the words of Jehoshaphat in 2 Chronicles 20:12, *"Neither know we what to do, but our eyes are on you."*

When we had truly committed her to God, then He went to work through the Holy Spirit.

There was a day when a friend of ours brought an enlarged photo of my husband taken during our summer youth camp. He brought it to the house just as I was on my way out . . . so I simply placed it on a chair near the back door.

Some time later, Lori came home, opened the door and noticed the picture as she walked by. Just as she reached the other door the Holy Spirit stopped her and spoke, like a shaft in her heart, these words, "If the Rapture takes place, that picture is all you will have left."

She later told us, after she had found a place of repentance, that moment was the turning place. It could only come as we carefully obeyed the Word of the Lord to give her over to Him in committal.

In the act of committing your teenage children to Christ, there is a place of complete relinquishment. *"Lord, they are yours. We have done all we can do as parents. We have set the example to the best of our ability and now they are in your hands. No longer will we preach, nag, scold, or threaten. Do with them according to your perfect will for their lives."*

Be ready for traumatic experiences . . . but let nothing they do or say cause you to waver. Remember, their lives have become the battleground between the forces of God and satan . . . but you have the promise of God that HE WILL PREVAIL.

7

Instrument Rated For Sickness

If we were to send out a questionnarie on what trouble visits people most frequently, or the trouble that is feared the most, the answer would come back doubtless, *sickness.*

Why?

Because it not only causes pain and discomfort, expense, and sorrow; but also it robs you of life. Many a robust, healthy person has been cut down in the zenith of life through the dread invasion of cancer, heart attack, or stroke.

This black, ominous cloud of sickness which knows no partiality, lies in wait for all. It comes suddenly and without prior warning. You feel a twinge of pain you have not felt before and it is abruptly there. You go to your physician for a routine yearly check-up. He listens to your heartbeat . . . then listens some more and begins to ask probing questions he has never asked before. Fear rises in your heart . . . and then the dreaded verdict comes.

You were not ready for it. Of all of the things remote in your thinking, this was the most far removed. You came from a family who all enjoyed long lives. You have never had a serious sickness in your whole life. This cannot be! There is no way you could be ready for this!

But there is a way to be ready for this storm of life . . . **a way that is not paved with fear** . . . a way that has so prepared the believer, that he can hear such a pronouncement from the physician and, simultaneously, have an immediate sense of peace pervade his heart. **He knows what the Bible, his instrument book, says about this storm of life.** He knows what to do, how to act, what to say. He is thoroughly prepared for that moment.

Even before the visit to the physician, when there were no storm clouds of symptoms on the horizon, he was preparing for the time when the instrument training would be put to the test. When trouble came, he was immediately ready to switch on to heavenly radar. This storm is sudden, but you have the equipment and the knowledge to fly right into the very teeth of this storm without fear.

Jesus, our Lord, must have experienced more compassion for this storm that comes against us than any other attack. He spent so much of His time healing the sick and ministering to the halt and lame. Great multitudes came to Him for healing and deliverance as virtue and power flowed out of Him in deliverance. God's attitude toward sickness is very vividly portrayed through Jesus, His Son. He does not want to see us suffer physically. He desires to see us in health.

His attitude is expressed so beautifully in 3 John 2: *"Beloved, I wish above all things that thou mayest prosper and be in health, even as thy soul prospereth."*

"And the Lord will take away from thee all sickness" (Deuteronomy 7:15a).

". . . And I will take sickness away from the midst of thee" (Exodus 23:25b).

". . . For I am the Lord that healeth thee" (Exodus 15:26c).

Most of the theology we have heard all of our lives casts great doubt as to God's position and attitude when it comes to this trial of our faith. We must have our doctrine straight here or our course through the storm will be fraught with uncertainties, doubt and fear.

Matthew 8:17 will help with this question. *"That it might be fulfilled which was spoken by Esaias the prophet, saying, Himself took our infirmities, and bare our sicknesses."*

Jesus, God's Son, healed all that came to Him. Never did He turn anyone down. The only ones who did not receive were those who came in unbelief. The lack of faith in His hometown of Nazareth kept Him from doing any great works there.

His attitude is always one of compassion, even to the extent that He took our sicknesses so that we would not have to bear them.

The Greek word for infirmities is "astheneia." It comes from the word "feebleness" meaning disease and sickness (Strong's Concordance). Literally, Jesus did something for us that we would not have the STRENGTH to do.

A human body cannot cope with viruses and germs. It must have help, either from natural or supernatural sources. The best source, of course, is divine help . . . but all good gifts are from God and this includes medical science. God knew how reliant we are and so Jesus, God's Son, took all of our physical infirmities upon himself.

God's attitude is very plainly stated. He is a God of compassion and healing. Believe it and act upon it.

Armed with this knowledge, you are ready to ward off this attack that is leveled at every child of God.

If you are an instrument rated Christian, you HAVE NOT WAITED for the attack before you prepared. You equipped yourself with many scriptures. You have been under the hood in simulated storm conditions. You are prepared to go by faith without visibly seeing or feeling. That will give you confidence. You are prepared to sit in total darkness just as the pilot sits in total darkness and observes only his gauges, radar and listens to his radio . . . believing what these instruments tell him. You now only believe what your instrument tells you. **You only believe the Scripture.** You do not listen to other voices or what your symptoms try to tell you. You are that "blessed" person that Jesus referred to when He said, "Blessed are those who believe who do not see."

You say, "Roy, I was not ready for that last battle I had with sickness. What can I do to be ready next time?"

To simulate a time of darkness when you cannot see or go by feelings is not easy. This is why many nominal, regular pilots do not proceed to get their instrument rating.

They say, "I can fly well and can go all of the places I want to go without it, so why should I spend the time and money when I may never need it?"

They may be right. But if they are wrong, just once . . . it could cost them their lives.

What you can do first is to have the desire to be ready. Be ready for any emergency, sickness or otherwise, by becoming very familiar with those passages you will be needing to know, i.e., being able to quote them, when the pain or symptoms signal loud and clear. Remember, above all things, you must speak (say aloud), not merely think the promises.

The power of the Word is in its being RELEASED THROUGH YOUR MOUTH.

"Faith comes by hearing" and it is you, hearing yourself say what God says about your condition that releases your faith. SAY WHAT GOD SAYS! Do not contradict your believing heart by what you say. Do not speak what you feel.

Men like Kenneth Hagin and myself will hear ourselves say, "Sickness, I refuse to believe your lying symptoms. I refuse to receive you and I rebuke you in the name of Jesus." Quoting the oracles of God is a powerful weapon in your hand. (Oracles are short, terse, sayings of God.)

I cannot be sick because You said You would bless my bread and water and take sickness away. (Exodus 23:25.)

You said You took our infirmities and bare our sicknesses. (Matthew 8:17.)

You said I could live unto righteousness by whose stripes I am healed. (1 Peter 2:24.)

You said You were the Lord that healeth all our diseases. (Psalm 103:3.)

Lord, I know this does not come from You, therefore I resist the one who sent it, satan. You said if I resist satan he will flee from me. (James 4:7.)

You need this special training, this simulated darkness, under the hood, when one can see only what the instrument, the Bible, says. Learning verses such as these is the training that will see you through the days when your pathway is obscured and symptoms are very real.

It is very important to know that we are not speaking of *positive thinking*.

Recently a very well known television minister, who constantly refers to the power of the mind, related this story.

It was during a time of very great stress and trial concerning a loved one who suffered a severe injury. This minister was overseas at the time and, upon hearing of the accident, caught the first flight to come home. During the flight there were several times when he was overcome and found it impossible to just sit silently. When he could sit still no longer, he would go back to the small restroom and lock the door. With the noise of the plane camouflaging his voice, HE WOULD CRY LOUDLY, "Hallelujah, hallelujah," until peace and confidence returned.

The power of the mind is not what people think it is. You may overcome some minor problems, but the serious storms can only be overcome by the POWER OF THE SPOKEN WORD OF GOD. That Word, flowing out of your mouth from the heart, will adequately prepare you for the inevitable trouble that will appear at your door saying, "Ready or not, here I am!"

YOU CAN BE READY!

8

Instrument Rated For Finances

All Christians, sooner or later, will be tested in the matter of finances. This storm comes also—ready or not. It will descend with a devastating attack when least expected.

Volumes have been written on financial problems and will continue to be written as long as money is the medium of exchange.

Just when you get ahead a little bit . . . something happens! Sometimes it is the car that needs repairs; sickness knocks; the house needs a new roof; the furnace or hot water tank gives up. You name it! We have all experienced it.

At the present time there seems to be some controversy and reaction to the prosperity message. Some have declared it to be an "American" doctrine and not taught in the Scripture. Some others think it is out of balance with the rest of Christianity in parts of the world where people go hungry and do not even have the bare necessities of life. This doctrine, as all others, ought to be approached strictly from the Scripture and not from practice or comparison with various cultures or ages.

The instrument rated pilot must have absolute confidence in his gauges, compass, and in his radio. If he looks at them and doubts their accuracy, he would be in serious difficulty. This all must be settled on the ground while he is going through the checklist. He cannot take off into the storm if all is not in good order.

Many Christians are flying their course of life and have not had a good check made of their craft— especially in money matters. They do not know what the Bible really says about their finances. They are not cognizant of God's attitude toward finances.

Thus, when the financial storm comes, they are forced out of their flight plan. They become grounded or end up at the wrong destination! They do not fly through, or above the storm because their flight plan was not settled before takeoff. They were not ready for this particular test.

What is God's attitude toward my financial status?

Does He want me to barely get along?

Does He want me to have just enough to make ends meet . . . or does He want me to be poor?

Does He want me to be prosperous? (By prosperous I mean having more than enough to meet my needs.)

God's attitude toward me is always to be considered in the light of knowing that **God is my Father.** *His attitude toward me is as a Father toward His child.*

What then, is my attitude toward my children on this earth?

Certainly, as it is with most parents, I want my children to have more than just enough to scrape through the day with. I want them to be free from worry about tomorrow. I want them to be prosperous. I am happy when they live in a nice house and drive a good car, eat good food, and wear nice clothing.

How can I attribute to my heavenly Father a less gracious attitude than I have toward my children? I would feel that I was sinning against God to do this.

God, as a Father, is best understood in His attitude toward His children, Israel. If we had no other teaching in Scripture than the 28th chapter of Deuteronomy, we would have enough to know His feelings about His children and finances.

"And all these blessings shall come on thee, and overtake thee, if thou shalt hearken (to hear diligently) *unto the voice of the Lord thy God"* (verse 2).

". . . and the Lord shall make thee plenteous (Hebrew yathar, to jut over, exceed, abound in goods)" (verse 11).

". . . and the Lord shall make thee the head and not the tail" (verse 13).

God has promised to bless them coming out and going in. All of these promises, of course, were conditional upon Israel obeying the Lord. Their history reveals that they did not obey and there is tragedy and destruction left in the wake of their disobedience.

The Bible says that the LOVE of money is the root of all evil in 1 Timothy 6:10. We are not to love to have money in an avaricious or miserly sense, but to have it for our needs.

To be blessed does not only means to have an overabundance of material wealth . . . but to be spiritually blessed as well.

The Greek word for salvation is "sozo." It means to deliver or protect, heal, preserve, do well, and be whole. Kittle says it means not only to be preserved and whole, but constantly replacing with new. It also means to remain in health; to be benefited.

When the Bible says, "Thou shalt be saved" in Romans 10:9, it means an all inclusive deliverance. God never intended His salvation to be only from sin, but also from poverty and ill health as well.

Galatians 3:9 says, "So then they which be of faith are blessed with faithful Abraham." The Greek word here for blessed is "eulogeo," meaning to prosper and be well off.

You must not only KNOW (have complete knowledge of what God says) but you must be READY for the storm of life. You cannot wait until the storm comes. You must be ready for it even as a pilot takes diligent training prior to the times he will need it. We must be constantly ready by speaking, quoting, these great truths over and over. Hear yourself repeating His Words before the test comes.

"My God wants me to prosper and be in health even as my soul prospers."

"He said He would bless me going out and coming in."

"The blessing of the Lord, it maketh rich, and He addeth no sorrow with it" (Proverbs 10:22).

"The young lions do lack and suffer hunger; but they that seek the Lord shall not want any good thing."

Regarding this last verse, the New English Bible says that unbelievers suffer, want, and grow hungry, but those who seek the Lord lack no good thing.

"He wants me to be in a place where there is no want of anything that is in the earth." (Judges 18:10.)

"The Lord is my shepherd, I shall not want" (Psalm 23:1).

"If I delight myself in the Lord, He will give me the desires of my heart." (Psalm 37:4.)

God said that if I give, He will give. *Giving is obedience.* You cannot expect God to have a generous attitude toward you, when your attitude is stingy and selfish. (I am assuming that this is thoroughly understood.)

God cannot do some things. If He did, He would not be a good God. To give a native in the jungle an air-conditioned Cadillac where there are not roads and gas is not available, would be ludicrous. In this case a bicycle or a horse would be equally beneficial and a great blessing.

There are some Christians in various parts of the world who would be greatly blessed just to have a plank floor to replace the dirt floor in their hut . . . or a motor for their dug-out canoe.

For some, just to get out of debt would make them feel like millionaries.

The doctrine of prosperity is world wide . . . but in perspective to people's needs.

Be ready for anything, but especially for trials that finances will put you through. You can be instrument rated for the storm. You can fly through it or above it. Know your instrument, file your flight plan with God. Get on heavenly radar. You are not going down . . . you are going up . . . sailing high above those ominous clouds . . . above the frustration and alarm of world economic conditions because you are a Christian.

The Christian Church fluctuates between the Cadillac syndrome and the poverty message. The balance is to know that God wants you to prosper and be in health EVEN AS YOUR SOUL PROSPERS.

Some faith teachers leave saints struggling to be rich, which turns to covetousness. This, in turn, can lead to greediness and the love of money. The other side leaves them with guilt when God does prosper them.

Psalm 35:27b says it very well. ". . . Yea let them say continually, let the Lord be magnified, which hath pleasure in the prosperity of his servant." (Prosperity can be translated to be "Peace, be whole.")

One is not at peace or whole if he is torn apart by financial disaster and trouble.

Don't let the extreme teacher on either side frustrate you. Some saints are not ready for a Cadillac . . . they are not even ready for a Volkswagon! Good faith teaching meets the believer where he is. It will not frustrate him by forcing him to strive for a higher level of faith than he is ready for.

When God says to His people that He will bless them coming in and going out, bless them in the city and in the country . . . He is talking about prosperity and peace. This is in the heart as well as in the pocketbook. Prosperity and peace in the home as well as in the office. Prosperity and peace in the body as well as in the soul.

Never doubt God's attitude toward your finances. He wants you to be in peace and that means abundance in all things. This knowledge will be the basic training for your instrument rating . . . for your financial flight through life.

Remember, God's economy is vastly different than that of the world. The motto of the world is "get all you can; get and save it for a rainy day." God's Word to us is, *"Give and it shall be given unto you, good measure, pressed down and shaken together and running over, shall men give into your bosom"* (Luke 6:38).

FAITH NEVER STRUGGLES—IT RESTS!

9

Instrument Rated For Old Wives' Fables

Recently I heard of a Hollywood film producer who drove himself relentlessly in his work and was a heavy user of marijuana and liquor. His revealed reason for doing this was, "Because I don't like to face the real world. It scares me."

If we really listen to what people are saying, we hear these same fears, anxieties, and worries constantly expressed. These are words of people who are totally reliant on their own resources and feelings, not comprehending the peace and confidence of the instrument rated Christian life. To the unsaved person, without God in this world, this is the way it is.

The *Humanist Manifesto*, the bible of the militant feminist, proclaims "There is no deity that can save us; we must save ourselves." That would be frightening, if it were true!

The only expressed fears and anxieties that really trouble me are the ones that fall from the lips of God's people—born-again Christians who have access to all of the powerful, revealed promises of God!

There is no doubt that *fear* is one of satan's most effective weapons . . . and he uses it profusely,

frightening people: in the physical realm with
symptoms and serious diagnoses of dread diseases; in
the mental realm with terrifying rumors and news
reports of the present and future.

I heard of a man, recently, that had willed various
parts of his body to be given to science when he died.
Then he heard about a life after death. He was
worried . . . fearful that if he came back, he would be
walking around with all of those parts missing!

Most despicable is the attempt of satan to strike
fear into the heart of a Christian who has declared
himself to be a child of God. If he can succeed in this,
he has not only caused great glee in the kingdom of
darkness, but he has also discouraged that fearful
Christian and any others who may have looked to him
for encouragement and support.

Some years ago, God gave me a great lesson on
the subject of fear during a brief visit in Managua,
Nicaragua. My son and I had traveled and seen things
of interest during the day; but now it was nighttime
and the missionary took us back to the guest room.
Roy Jr. was 11 years old at the time.

The guest room was a small adobe room at the
back of the compound. He warned us to be sure and
bolt the door and close the wooden shutters because it
was not uncommon to have thieves climb over the
walls at night. We did as he said.

As I was preparing to put out the light, I glanced
toward the ceiling. In the corner of the room, high and
out of reach, was a very large South American spider!

There was no way I could reach it. We spent a fitful, sleepless and jittery night—imaginations working overtime.

Day finally came and with it the missionary. I showed him the spider which had not moved, despite all of our imaginary sensations, in the night. He said, "I'll take care of that." He stepped outside, came back in with a long stick and reached up to crush the spider. The moment he touched it, it disintegrated into hundreds of particles floating to the ground. You see, the spider was dead, dried and only the form of it remained!

In that moment I said, "Thank you Lord, that is probably one of the greatest lessons about fear that I will ever have."

Think about all of the things you have ever feared, been anxious about or dreaded. *Haven't they been imagined? off in the future? specters of someone's discouraging words or, as it was with me, fears that stemmed from ignorance?*

Because the subject matter of this book tends to deal with being prepared for trouble that comes our way as a result of being in the devil's world (2 Corinthians 4:4 says that "the god of this world has blinded the minds of them that believe not"), I would like to explore a topic that is applicable to every woman's life experience. This is a subject where we tend to find much fear and apprehension. We can deal only with the subject from a biblical basis, not being qualified to write from medical perspective.

Recently I talked with a friend. In the course of our conversation, she mentioned a friend of hers, in her late 40's facing the menopause. She was facing it filled with dread, making such statements as, "I would rather die than go through it." and "I want someone to lock me in a closet when that time comes."

If this was the only time I had ever heard statements like these . . . or if this was a rare instance . . . then we could pass them off as that. But the truth is that we hear them over and over, and thousands of women are locked into a fear of this normal body process.

Symptomatic of this fear of the menopause, and of the aging that it heralds, are the tens of thousands of women who take estrogen. In doing this, they have only traded one fear for another because of the widespread knowledge of studies such as a 1979 study at the University of Pennsylvania. It revealed that users of estrogen are six times more likely to have uterine cancer than non-users. Many women take it more for psychological benefit than for physical good. They believe it will "ward off" the encroachment of the aging process and that they will feel and look younger.

We are not preparing a case against estrogen. We are presenting what the Bible says about the very natural, reasonable, and essential aging process. When we understand what the Bible says about it, then it becomes not only natural and reasonable, but we can anticipate and look forward to it without artificial means to help us bear it. Gradual aging comes to us all and is not to be feared.

Mother Humbard replied to someone who mentioned her age, "Sure I am getting older. If I wasn't I'd be dead!"

John Wesley, at 71 said, "I find just the same strength as I did thirty years ago . . . my sight is considerably better now, and my nerves firmer. I have none of the infirmities of old age and have lost several I had in my youth!"

These are words of people who are instrument rated to fly through storms of old wives' fables and myths. What we see here is the therapeutic and positive affect of right thinking and right talking.

Aging, and the bodily changes that come with it, are all a part of God's plan and are to be accepted . . . knowing that as Christians we are free from the curse of sickness and affliction.

If you are older and the menopause is already a part of your past, then this chapter will not be as significant for you as it is for those approaching it. If you are very young, then tuck this word away in the recesses of your memory against the future.

The first Word of God to me as that time of my own life approached was a portion of 1 Timothy 4:7: "Refuse profane and old wives' fables." This verse, quite frankly, had nothing to do with this female physical experience. But it effectively taught a truth and a principle that is significant in dealing with this tool of satan.

How many times have you heard statements like these?

"When the menopause comes, your mind goes."

"Your husband won't love you anymore."

"You won't be able to remember anything."

"You'll be susceptible to all kinds of physical trouble."

On and on . . . ad infinitum!

What kind of authenticity do they have? NONE. These are only the "old wives' fables," the fiction, the tales that are told from generation to generation.

God's truth is that we need never "fear their fear, nor be afraid" (Isaiah 8:12). Their fears cannot become ours *without our permission*. We are the custodians of our will, emotions, and our bodies.

If God says, "Be not afraid of sudden fear," as He does in Proverbs 3:25, then it must be within the realm of our capability to resist fear. He does not require something of us that we cannot do.

He is a kind, compassionate heavenly Father. He wants us to be strong and enjoy all of the benefits of living in His family. Being free of fear is one of these great benefits.

If satan knocks at your door and says, "You've enjoyed a good life up to this point, but look out now . . . that's all going to change. From now on it's all down hill. Your mind and body will deteriorate and your usefulness will end"; look him right in the eye and say, "Devil, Psalm 91:16 says that God will SATISFY me with long life and show me His salvation. A SATISFYING life is a sound, healthy, wholesome life—whole and entire." That is what belongs to the woman of God!

Instead of becoming immobile, of vegetating, it is very important that we keep active. Our mental capacities do not cease because of the menopause . . . neither do sexual interests, creative interests and the desire to be involved with life. A reasonable program of activity will do much to extend the fulfillment of those contented years.

Instead of looking for the disabilities that have been associated with this physical process, begin to look for compensations. It can continue to be a time of growing and learning . . . free of many former pressures.

In Psalm 139:13-16, the formation of the body in the womb is described. It shows the meticulous supervision of God to the minutest detail, the greatest of care. Verse 13 speaks of our being "covered," protected, defended, even as in the mother's womb. In verse 15 where it says we were "curiously wrought" the Hebrew word "rukkamti" means *embroidered, made of needlework* and describes the intricate formation of the body.

Adam Clarke's Commentary says of verse 15, "As the embroiderer has still his work pattern, before him, to which he always refers; so, by a method as exact, were all my members in continuance fashioned, i.e., from the rude skeins of variously colored silk or worsted, under the artificer's hands, there at length arises an unexpected beauty, and an accurate harmony of colors and proportions."

His careful attention to the nerves, blood vessels, tendons as they are curiously wrought as intricate embroidery or needlework is as it would be done by the hand of an artist. The God who so carefully watches over the formation of the body in the womb, will continue to cover, protect and defend me through my life's growth and experience. He will do this because He has promised to do so. I declare His promise.

Psalm 37 is full of strong, positive words to declare.

"Trust in the Lord and do good, so shalt thou dwell in the land, and verily thou shalt be fed."

"Delight thyself in the Lord and He shall give thee the desires of thine heart."

"The Lord knoweth the days of the upright; and their inheritance shall be forever."

"The salvation of the righteous is of the Lord; He is their strength in the time of trouble."

There are approximately 3,000 promises in the Word, all for our benefit. God wants us to use them!

When symptoms of any physical problems that are due to menopause or the aging process come, I have learned to say. *"Greater is He that is in me than he that is in the world"* (I John 4:4). *"I am more than a conqueror through Him that loved me"* (Romans 8:37). My physical body has never failed to respond to that confession of His Word.

When these fears knock at your door, answer by saying, **"God promised that He would satisfy me with long life. A satisfied life is a long, full, rich life free from fear and sickness and old wives' fables."**

10
Instrument Rated For Growing Older

You may have glanced at some of the chapter headings and thought that some of them did not apply to you, but this chapter is one that fits us all. Has anyone in history ever been ready for old age? Has its long tentacles steadily reached out, slowly engulfing us until one day, we suddenly realized we were at that time of life?

Little things we had always done have now become a chore. You wanted to walk to the store, but a ride sounded better. You knew you should walk those three flights of steps but the elevator was quicker. You tried jogging but a few blocks did you in. You had so slowly adjusted that you either did not notice or your subconscious would not permit you to face up to the truth. You had reached that time of life! For many this is not only a very traumatic, emotional experience, but one from which they never fully recover.

This inevitable storm need not be one for which we are not prepared. It need not catch you by surprise. Let it be one storm you can be fully prepared to fly right into, rising above it and enjoying every one of your golden years.

You might ask, "How can I become a fully instrumented Christian . . . one who is ready for this unavoidable flight of aging?"

The earlier you start preparation, the smoother the flight will be. But, regardless of your present age, YOU CAN BEGIN NOW.

Our instrument, the Bible, has all of the answers to all of life's storms. The storm of aging or growing older is no exception. We can begin with the beautiful, satisfying words of our Lord Jesus: ". . . and lo, I am with you alway, even to the end of the world" (Matthew 28:20b). Yes, our Lord and Savior promised to never leave us or forsake us.

The believing Christian not only has a good life when he is young, but even to the very end.

When do we begin to claim these promises? Is it when we see the first gray hairs? When we are presented with our first grandchild? When a young person comes up to us and says that we remind him of his father instead of his brother?

DON'T WAIT FOR THESE EXPERIENCES! Begin now to confess your enjoyment of every birthday you will celebrate. Don't say such things as, "I am 39 and holding," as though you are afraid to face one more year. Rather say what the Psalmist said, "I have been young and now I am old(er) yet have I not seen the righteous forsaken nor his seed begging bread" (Psalm 37:25).

The main fear of getting older, whether it is a conscious fear or a subconscious one, is the *fear of being alone, needy, and un-needed.* In these days of inflation, when soaring prices dwindle the resources of the pension check, how sustaining it is to be able to confess that not only will my Lord NOT FORSAKE ME, but HE WILL SUPPLY MY EVERY NEED. Old age is to be the crowning era of our lives! Proverbs 16:31 says, "The hoary head is a crown of glory." Even if we are forsaken by loved ones, we are not alone. The Lord will take us up. (Psalm 27:10.)

These older years can be the most blessed years of our lives, spiritually. In fact, all of the things you wanted to do and didn't have time to do when you were younger are open and available now. Didn't you always say, "I wish I had more time to read?" Now you can. Have you said, "I wish I had more time to spend in prayer and Bible reading?" Now you can. So many things: travel, hobbies, visiting friends . . . now you have the time to enjoy them.

Job 5:26 speaks of going to the grave in a full age. Judges 8:32 speaks of a good old age. Genesis 25 speaks of old men, full of years. Think of all of these statements. This can be said of you. You can come to a place of full age, a good, old age . . . and die full of years.

I know of a Christian who said all during his lifetime, "I don't want to live beyond my 80th birthday. By that time, I will have enjoyed life. I will have done all I wanted to do, seen all I wanted to see, and been everywhere I wanted to go. I will be ready to go on and be with my Lord." He was saying that he would have reached a full age, a good old age, and be ready to die full of years.

Few reach that place. Most give up. They sit and do nothing instead of reaching out, taking on new projects, making new friends, learning new hobbies, venturing into new ministries. There have been a few people who have taken their pension and volunteered to do missionary work in a foreign field. There is the option of doing Red Cross work or volunteer work for your church.

So many challenges await your golden years. Years of experience need not be wasted. You have much to offer now . . . and even more as the years add to your wisdom and abilities.

Notice that God never has a generation gap. "Then shall the virgin rejoice in the dance, both young men and old together . . ." (Jeremiah 31:13a). "One generation shall praise thy works to another" (Psalm 145:4).

Being instrument rated for old age is simply being prepared for that time of life by memorizing and becoming familiar with the great passages of Scripture.

Here is a good one: *"And even to your old age I am he; and even to hoar hairs will I carry you: I have made and I will bear; even I will carry and deliver you"* (Isaiah 46:4).

"Thus saith the Lord of hosts, there shall yet old men and old women dwell in the streets of Jerusalem

and every man with his staff in his hand for very age"
(Zechariah 8:4).

*"Cast me not off in the time of old age, forsake me
not when my strength faileth. Now also when I am old
and gray headed, Oh God forsake me not: until I have
shewed thy strength unto this generation and thy
power to everyone that is to come. Thou shalt increase
my greatness and comfort me on every side"* (Psalm
71:9,18,21).

Growing older graciously is available for every
child of God. We need not fear old age. Sometimes we
gloss over a growing uneasiness about approaching
age. We joke about it in an attempt to "cover up" our
real feelings.

Like the lady buying a hat. She tried one on and
her friend said, "My that makes you look ten years
younger."

She put the hat back on the shelf quickly saying,
"I don't want that one . . . I'd hate to look ten years
older every time I took it off!"

This is one storm of life that we have every
opportunity of being prepared for. It is one that cannot
come upon us unaware! We will not be engulfed in this
storm, helpless and afraid. It will not hinder or cripple
us but, in fact, will be a great blessing both to us and
those around us.

Let the last words of that great eighth chapter of
Romans be your "glide slope" that will take you to a
successful landing . . . even if the runway is obscured.

"Who shall separate us from the love of Christ? Shall tribulation, or distress, or persecution or famine, or nakedness, or peril or sword? As it is written, for thy sake we are killed all the day long; we are accounted as sheep for the slaughter. Nay in all these things we are more than conquerors through him that loved us. For I am persuaded that neither death, nor life, nor angels, nor principalities, nor powers, nor things present, nor things to come, nor height, nor depth, nor any other creature, shall be able to separate us from the love of God which is in Christ Jesus our Lord."

Most young people always seek out an older person, full of wisdom and experience, for counsel and guidance. You can be that person who has matured gracefully. You can be full of wisdom and the Holy Spirit. Begin to seek God.

Serve God in such a way that when that time of life comes, you can answer the door and say, "I am ready for you. I am instrumented to go all the way. I will be a greater blessing in my golden years than I was in my youth. I am ready."

11

Instrument Rated For Bad News

Second Kings 19:14 reads, "And Hezekiah received the letter of the hand of the messenger and read it; and Hezekiah went up into the house of the Lord, and spread it before the Lord."

All people of the earth, even kings, will be the recipient of bad news.

Sometimes the message comes by letter, sometimes by phone. Many times it has been the sound of screeching tires and broken glass. Bad news knows no class lines, partiality, sex, or age. It breaks upon all.

King Hezekiah did what we should all do when bad news is received. **He spread it out before the Lord.** Take it to Him, not second, but first. God is a God of first things. When trouble comes to you, do not put Him second . . . put Him first.

"But seek ye first the Kingdom of God and His righteousness and all these things shall be added unto you" (Matthew 6:33).

Many people make an unwise decision to seek out a friend, a doctor or lawyer, BEFORE they (first) spread it out before the Lord.

The Greek word for "seek," in Matthew 6:33, is "zeteo": it means to "inquire and require." This means that when I seek, or inquire of the Lord concerning my problem, there is an automatic *requirement* of the Lord to do something about it. It is not that man makes the requirement; it is the result of God's promise to man when he inquires.

So many times when we fail to put God first, we not only remove Him to second position in our lives; but we remove Him from taking part in our time of crisis.

To "inquire" means you seek him FIRST!

God is a God of first things. "In the beginning God!" He is first. To seek Him first in our times of testing means that we highly honor Him as the Lord God, the Eternal One. When we do not put Him first, we do not honor Him as the Supreme One, the Alpha, the God of Genesis 1:1.

To make a habit of seeking God first, whether there is a crisis or not, is a hallmark of the instrument rated Christian.

Recently a large jet aircraft crash landed in a heavily populated area of our city. Miraculously, not many people were killed. One woman remarked about how lucky the survivors were. When she was reminded of the testimonies of the surviving people who were fervently praying moments before the crash, she said, "Well, yes, prayer . . . but at a time like that?!"

It was true, that when the Christians aboard the plane knew the plane was in trouble and the stewardess had instructed them in crash preparation, they immediately turned to God and prayed. They believe God gave them a great miracle. Not only were all but just a few people saved without injury, but the two houses that were destroyed in that heavily populated area were empty ones. It pays to immediately turn to the Lord.

To be an instrument rated Christian means you have prepared yourself to receive bad news. You are not looking for it. You do not believe for it or confess it. But facing the reality of knowing you are living in the devil's world, prepares you to deal with its negatives.

Most people will REACT IN PANIC when they hear of calamities that affect them personally. They are not ready, not prepared for the storm. They are overwhelmed, not knowing which way to turn.

If a regularly licensed pilot flies into a fog bank, vertigo sets in. He has not been trained to fly by his instruments, so he is disoriented and confused. All commercial pilots, being responsible for many lives, fly only by instruments. They are constantly watched over by radar centers. These centers know exactly where that plane is and they know if trouble is near. They are ready at all times for trouble.

An instrument rated Christian is ready at all times for bad news because he is constantly setting his course with the help of the heavenly radar. *He has*

*prepared himself by knowing what the instrument, the
Word of God, has to say about trouble.*

He knows that Romans 8:28 is true. He knows
that all things do work together for good to them that
love God.

When trouble or bad news comes, he does not say,
"I don't know what I am going to do." He says, "I
don't understand this but, by faith, I know it will work
out all right." He is prepared because he is constantly
confessing this. He is an instrument rated Christian
. . . prepared for any eventuality of life.

Much of the bad news we hear is a result of other
people's problems. Sometimes, when we hear of them,
they become our problems. I fervently believe that we
are to help one another: to pray on for the other and
help with the "overload." But there are times when
the world "dumps" its problem load on us. We allow
the news media to depress us when we hear of the
catastrophic world news, as well as the sorrow and
tragedy of our nation and neighborhoods. We begin to
worry and fret over all of these problems. This not
only fails to help the trouble, but it causes us harm.

The authors react to the negatives of life around
them **by speaking the Word of God that will fit that
occasion,** and then refusing again to refer to that
particular problem or circumstance. Mulling it over or
spreading it abroad only aggravates and keeps alive
things that are better off forgotten.

Hezekiah, in taking the bad news to the Lord first, taught us all by his example what to do when trouble comes our way.

I heard of a mother who received a telegram from the army that said her son was killed in action. She took the telegram and spread it out before the Lord, along with her Bible. She said, "This telegram says my son is dead. Your Word promises me that anything I ask in Your name You will do. I can either believe Your Word, or the telegram. I CHOOSE to believe Your Word."

She then sent to the army a telegram that read, "You must be mistaken. My son cannot be dead."

After hasty and more thorough searching, they sent another telegram saying, "You are correct. Your son is alive. There was a case of mistaken identity."

This dear saint of God was truly instrument rated. She was prepared for trouble. She knew God and His Word.

You also can be prepared for bad news by knowing God and knowing what He says about any dilemma or critical situation you will ever have to face—even death. Remember, the very worst thing that can happen to you is death . . . *which is the greatest thing that can happen!* To be absent from the body is to be present with the Lord!

One thing to remember when you hear bad news is to not allow the mind to make it worse than it actually is. Be sure you wait until all the facts are in before you make a judgment.

We have learned much about "negative reporting." So many times we receive a very negative report concerning the weather we are going to fly through. Most of the time it is not as bad as it sounds. Many times there are several hundred feet of clear weather in between the layers of storm clouds. We are actually BETWEEN TROUBLE, flying safely along when all around us is stormy.

Remember to take that negative report which can be true (or have some truth in it) and spread it out before the Lord. He saw you going through this a long time before you knew anything about it. You can say, "Father, I thank You that You knew this would happen before I did. Whatever You see necessary for me to do to OVERCOME this, show me; for I trust in You and believe this will work out for Your glory."

An airplane pilot goes through a very thorough checklist before taking off on his trip. Why not begin each day of your life by saying something TO God, the first thing each morning. Some people say, "Good Lord, it's morning!" instead of "Good morning, Lord." Let your first words of the day be TO YOUR LORD.

Then, each day be sure you say something to somebody ABOUT God. (Malachi 3:16 talks about the book God is writing . . . filling it with the things you say to others.) This keeps you constantly aware of His presence. Thus, you are always ready for bad news when it comes.

Then, every day repeat something GOD HAS SAID ABOUT YOU. This keeps you speaking His Word. This keeps you instrument rated.

12

Instrument Rated For Death

". . . And it is appointed (destined) unto men once to die" (Hebrews 9:27a).

". . . For we must needs die, and are as water spilt on the ground" (2 Samuel 14:14a).

"For I know that thou wilt bring me to death, and to the house appointed for all living" (Job 30:23).

"My dwelling is removed, and is carried away from me as a shepherd's tent" (Isaiah 38:12 RV).

"Whereas ye know not what shall be on the morrow. For what is your life? It is even a vapour, that appeareth for a little time and then vanisheth away" (James 4:14).

To quote many verses about death would surely not be necessary. Don't we all know we are going to die? Yes, we do . . . but we don't. This is a paradox. Perhaps it stems from hazy memories from childhood of the death of a friend or loved one. It comes to be something we *know*, but won't *acknowledge*. We may flippantly mention it . . . but will not dwell on it.

Before we leave the impression that this chapter on the subject of being ready for death contradicts the basic, inherent desire that God gives us to want to live, let me first establish this great truth. We thank God for the incentive to live.

It would be a heavy burden for one to carry through life, to continually be thinking, "Today I might die" . . . to be constantly monitoring your vital signs, looking for signs of failing!

This fervent desire to live and survive is one of God's special gifts to us. There are so many people who, in a fit of depression, commit suicide now; what would it be if this protection were not built into us? One shudders to think of it. This God-given gift that causes us to fight off death, prolonging even the suffering of it, to cling to life a little longer, has caused many of God's own family to come abruptly face to face with death and find they are not prepared for it.

How can we possibly be instrument rated to face this ominous storm cloud unless we are as death-conscious as we are life-conscious? This is not an easy assignment, but it is a very necessary one.

First, let us prepare ourselves for the death of others. Your close family members, your close friends . . . any of these could die at any moment. Are you ready for that telegram, that phone call? Would you be prepared to answer the door and find a policeman standing there with a death message? Are you prepared, spiritually equipped, so that you could receive such news and still proceed with the demands and routine of daily living?

The instrument rated pilot must be prepared for a crash landing—the worst thing that can happen. He does not fear it, or talk about it, but he must be ready. This author flies many thousands of miles in jet liners. Prior to takeoff, the flight crew prepares the passengers for emergencies by pointing out the escape exits and survival techniques.

Can we use our imaginations?

What would it be like if every pastor would precede his sermons with the words, "Now, as we begin this service, let me once again warn you that you are just one heartbeat from eternity and at any moment you may feel pain around your heart. Be ready! If you are not ready, just call out to God anytime during the service." People would not tolerate this and the pastor would soon be speaking to empty pews. We just do not want to hear about dying.

Accusers are quick to say, "scare tactics" when the subject is mentioned. No one can prepare you to be ready. You must assume this responsibility. You must be prepared for its advent—unthinkable as it is.

There is no way the sinner can be prepared. Many of them talk lightly and jest about it. You hear these remarks: "When you're dead, you're dead"; "When your time comes to go, you go"; "What is to be, will be."

The most difficult time for any honest clergyman is to conduct a funeral for someone that died without hope.

IF YOU ARE READING THIS BOOK AND YOU DO NOT KNOW JESUS AS YOUR SAVIOR, YOU

CAN ONLY BE READY FOR DEATH BY RECEIV-
ING HIM AS YOUR LORD AND SAVIOR.

Then, on that day, you can hear Him say:
"Blessed are the dead which die in the Lord from
henceforth: Yea, saith the Spirit, that they may rest
from their labours; and their works do follow them."

As Pastor Jerry Cook so ably puts it, "We mourn
at the grave when, in fact, we should rejoice. Just as
the womb of our mother births life to the flesh . . . so
death releases us from the life of that flesh into a new
continuing series of beginnings."

Being instrument rated for death not only
prepares you, but surely helps those who are left
behind. When they look upon your form, they can
stand and rejoice knowing you were ready. It makes it
easier for them to face life without you and to look
forward to that great reunion with you and with our
Lord.

Jesus said, *"I am the resurrection and the life. He
that believeth in me though he were dead yet shall he
live."*

To contact Roy and Margaret Hicks,
write:

Roy and Margaret Hicks
P. O. Box 4113
Lake San Marcos, California 92069

*Feel free to include your prayer requests
and comments when you write.*

Books By Dr. Roy H. Hicks

Keys of the Kingdom

The Power of Positive Resistance
The Christian's Antihistamine

Healing Your Insecurities

Praying Beyond God's Ability
Why Prayers Go Unanswered

Use It Or Lose It
The Word of Faith

He Who Laughs Lasts . . . And Lasts . . . And Lasts

Another Look At The Rapture

Whatever Happened To Hope

Obtaining Bible Promises —
A Different Approach for Every Promise

Available at your local bookstore.

HARRISON HOUSE
P. O. Box 35035 • Tulsa, Oklahoma 74153

PRAYING BEYOND GOD'S ABILITY

by Dr. Roy Hicks

Learn the principles of true prayer. Many believers experience frustrations and feelings of deep condemnation because of their misunderstanding regarding unanswered prayer.

This is a book that will bring you to face the reality of unanswered prayers and help you to do something about it.